Interiors *in* Blue

ROCKPORT

ROCKPORT PUBLISHERS

GLOUCESTER, MASSACHUSETTS

First published in the United States of America by:
Rockport Publishers, Inc.
33 Commercial Street
Gloucester, Massachusetts 01930-5089
Telephone: (978) 282-9590
Facsimile: (978) 283-2742

Distributed to the book trade and art trade in the United States by:
North Light Books, an imprint of
F & W Publications
1507 Dana Avenue
Cincinnati, Ohio 45207
Telephone: (800) 289-0963

Other Distribution by:
Rockport Publishers, Inc.
Gloucester, Massachusetts 01930-5089

ISBN 1-56496-441-8

10 9 8 7 6 5 4 3 2 1

Designer: Karen Rappaport
Cover Image: Interior Design by Growing Spaces: Marcia Connors and
          Roxy Gray
          Photo by Steve Vierra
          See page 45

Printed in Hong Kong by Midas Printing Limited.

For more beautiful work by the designers and photographers featured in this collection, please see:

Showcase of Interior Design: Eastern Edition 1
Showcase of Interior Design: Eastern Edition 2
Showcase of Interior Design: Eastern Edition 3
Showcase of Interior Design: Midwest Edition 1
Showcase of Interior Design: Midwest Edition 2
Showcase of Interior Design: Pacific Edition 1
Showcase of Interior Design: Pacific Edition 2
Showcase of Interior Design: Southern Edition 1
Showcase of Interior Design: Southern Edition 2
Colors for Living: Bedrooms by Carol Meredith
Colors for Living: Living Rooms by Jennie Pugh
Eclectic Style in Interior Design by Carol Meredith

Blue: the color of the ocean, the color of the sky. From faded blue jeans to sapphires, blue is all around us. Each different shade of blue will draw a different emotional response from you. Pale blues will add a sense of tranquillity, a peace not found in the starkness of plain white. Bright blues will energize a room, especially in combination with the other primary colors, red and yellow. Blues and greens mixed in different shades and variations will recall a sunny tropical ocean or the pale serenity of a summer meadow. Blue lends itself to patterns, from the popular gingham to delft china. The color alone will not create the total effect. Shiny blue surfaces will reflect the light and create a different effect than a matte or textured surface. Consider the natural and unnatural light sources that will surround blue in a living room, or the shaded light that appears in a bedroom. Light and texture factor into the final appearance of the color. From accent pillows to furniture to walls to curtains, in flat washes or intricate patterns, blue can be the perfect choice of color for every room of the home. The choice depends on you.

(above) A 1970s house with dark pine post-and-beam construction, rough cedar, and moss rock was renovated into an airy contemporary residence highlighting expansive views of the mountains in Snowmass, Colorado. Evening sunsets cast blue and purple hues, inspiring the use of rich jewel tones against a light background.

(right) Original 4x4 posts were sheathed in drywall to form large columns and connected with a glass wall in the dining room to enhance privacy. The contemporary Navajo weaving above the fireplace adds to the regional uniqueness of the space.

INTERIOR DESIGN
Sara Zook Designs, Ltd.

(opposite page) INTERIOR DESIGN
Riemenschneider Design Associates, Inc.

(right) Cool blue fabric offers a soothing corner for reading and relaxation.

INTERIOR DESIGN

Judith Lynne Interior Design

(below) An eclectic room, warm and inviting. The built-in units conceal a large screen television and a multitude of storage.

INTERIOR DESIGN

Peter Charles Interiors

(above and left) Mirrors enlarge the living and dining areas which have an art deco influence alive with color and exotic traditional accents.

INTERIOR DESIGN
Rhonda A. Roman Interiors
Detriot, Michigan

(above) Elements of the British "Raj" in India accentuate this sun-filled garden room. A settee and chair of carved, painted teak provide seating around a faux leopard-skin floorcloth; a screen depicting European neo-classic architecture forms a backdrop amid a variety of plants.

INTERIOR DESIGN
Horne International Designs, Inc.

(left) INTERIOR DESIGN
Blair Design Associates, Inc.

(above) An eclectic mix of silks, velvets, linens, and taffetas enhances unusual furnishings and accessories throughout the salon. A theatrical Andrew Dubreuil iron and glass torchiere is set against a backdrop of a mirror and satin and taffeta curtains.

INTERIOR DESIGN
Dennis Rolland, Inc.

(right) Motoakasaka House, Fukuoka, Japan

INTERIOR DESIGN
Ronald Bricke & Associates, Inc.

(left and below) INTERIOR DESIGN

Jane J. Marsden Antiques & Interiors, Inc.

(left) INTERIOR DESIGN

Mary W. Delany Interior Design

13

A limited palette—here, a few blue tones and crisp white—can provide richness and depth. The distinctive color scheme and billowing fabric are familiar and comforting, like blue and white delft.

INTERIOR DESIGN
Glenna Cook, ASID
Photo: Russell Abraham

(opposite page) An artistic design element sets the stage for an expansive living area.

INTERIOR DESIGN
Susan Fredman & Associates, Ltd.

(right) One of Addison Mizner's 1922 oceanfront mansions, this Palm Beach, Florida, residence features an addition that's historically accurate but furnished for today's lifestyle.

INTERIOR DESIGN
Stedila Design, Inc.

(below) A classic modern house, built in 1960, restored to its original splendor with a new liveability. The rug is an original design by Annie Albers, artist and wife of Josef Albers, the famous color theorist.

INTERIOR DESIGN
David Ripp Incorporated

(above) A dining room in a Federal house features antique furniture, drawings by Robert Motherwell, and custom carpeting by Stark.

INTERIOR DESIGN
Carl Steele Associates, Inc.

(above) A blue antique robe and exquisite Chinese procelains punctuate an otherwise neutral living room.

INTERIOR DESIGN

Ginny Stine Interiors, Inc.

(right) An Eastern sitting room shows influence of Moroccan and Turkish ornaments and architecture.

INTERIOR DESIGN

Horne International Designs, Inc.

(opposite page) INTERIOR DESIGN

Carl Steele Associates, Inc.

(above) Strong architectural details in the fireplace and windows set the mood for this comfortable living room. Tiered gardens of flowers reflect the soft palette inside, while walnut floors underscore the soft warmth of the pastel Oriental rugs and Chinese porcelains.

INTERIOR DESIGN
Sara Zook Designs, Ltd.

(right) The lacquered screen and Chinese flower pots incorporate more subtle versions of the vivid color palette of this space.

INTERIOR DESIGN
Robert E. Tartarini Interiors

Photo: Dennis Krukowski

(above) The metal and wood blend
of the tables, contemporary lines of
the furniture, and narrow shelf along
the wall displaying old treasures,
such as a scale and wooden boxes,
work well together.

INTERIOR DESIGN
Mark Zeff

Photo: Mario Ruiz

(above) In the living room of this residence, a collection of framed images is given emphasis mounted on a blue-tinted glass mirror. Vintage bowling balls from the 1940s are treated like moveable pieces of art.

(left) In the dining room, a collection of Robert Mapplethorpe photographs are juxtaposed with a pop-art cabinet with custom-designed buffet wings. The colors of the cabinet and buffet are picked up in the horizontal stripes of the crown molding, which is painted to resemble the coat of a Dalmatian.

INTERIOR DESIGN
Al Evans Interiors
Photos: Dan Forer

(above) The offices of an investment firm provide residential elegance and comfort without sacrificing efficiency and durability.

INTERIOR DESIGN
Solis-Betancourt

(right) Note how the palm tree and blue door frames add splashes of color to a living space that relies on simple, comfortable white furnishings.

INTERIOR DESIGN
C. M. Wright, Inc.

(below) Renovating a room not part of a historical house, the designer aimed for a contemporary nautical feeling more conductive to its summer residents. Previously dark, this room is now much lighter in feeling, with whisper white walls.

INTERIOR DESIGN
Alexis E. Benné Interiors

(top right) The owner of this Southampton, NY farmhouse wanted to display a collection of Russian furnishings and accessories in a formal environment. The yellow and blue color scheme goes from the palest shade of yellow to brilliant blue in a sophisticated take on a tried-and-true color combination.

(bottom right) This dramatic salon for a famous New York modern art dealer was designed to complement a vibrant collection of art. The room rates a variety of unique and luxurious finishes created by a talented group of artisans, including a graphite ceiling and pigmented beeswax encaustic walls. The daring jewel-tone color scheme was inspired by the Stephen Mueller painting over the sofa.

INTERIOR DESIGN
Dennis Rolland, Inc.

(right) This eclectic living room was designed to highlight the client's collection of Oriental antiques.

INTERIOR DESIGN

Arlis Ede Interiors, Inc.

(below) INTERIOR DESIGN

Susan Kroeger, Ltd.

(opposite page) Deep reds and blues accented by royal gold tones envelope a stately study.

INTERIOR DESIGN

William R. Eubanks Interior Design

(above) Hand-painted seafoam-blue stripes add a touch of whimsy to a formal entry foyer. The designer's favorite antique pink luster adds color to a demilune console.

INTERIOR DESIGN
Elizabeth Read Weber, ASID, LLC

(top right) A combination library and formal family room offers a palette inspired by the 1930s Morharjean Sarouk rug. The custom cherry woodwork creates a warm and inviting living area.

INTERIOR DESIGN
Julie Lanterman Interior Designs

(bottom right) This room was originally a music room. It no longer hears the sound of a piano, but it is a cheerful, engulfing room done in toile, colonial blue, and gingham, mixed with sunlight. A great room to daydream in.

INTERIOR DESIGN
Alexis E. Benné Interiors

(below) Vibrant crayon colors electrify this living room, helping to brighten a home situated in a canyon.

INTERIOR DESIGN

Tomar Lampert Associates

(above) Purchase the highest quality pieces your budget will allow—it will be less expensive in the long run.

INTERIOR DESIGN
Tonin MacCallum ASID, Inc.

(above) An exercise and enter-
tainment area for a home sports
center boasts every possible
amenity, from a full-sized billiard
table to a private massage
room.

INTERIOR DESIGN
Horne International Designs, Inc.

Old World 17th century
Mediterranean style living
room combining all countries
and cultures.

INTERIOR DESIGN
Fetzer's Interiors

(left) IDeep copper and regal blue complement the wood paneling and percelain in this music room.

INTERIOR DESIGN

Akins and Aylesworth, Ltd.

(right) The grand living room of a Hudson River property projects designer Barbara Ostrom's ability to recreate period architecture, cabinetry, columns and mouldings while orchestrating color, texture, fabrics, and furnishings in a large scale setting.

INTERIOR DESIGN
Barbara Ostrom Associates

(left) Traditional New Orleans
Garden District formal parlor.

INTERIOR DESIGN
Fetzer's Interiors

(above) The designer worked with Gauguin-like colors such as greens, purples, and marigolds to provide a sheltered environment for this glass and limestone pavilion-like space. Softly upholstered cushion-
ing on a platform became the dividing space
between the living room. The contemporary, oriental
design creates casual elegance.

INTERIOR DESIGN
Rita St. Clair Associates, Inc.

(above) INTERIOR DESIGN

Robert Pope Associates, Inc.

(left and below) INTERIOR DESIGN

G. M. Doveikis & Associates, Inc.

Photo: Fentress Photography

(above) Intelligent furniture
placement creates a number
of distinct functional areas in
a visually intriguing space.

INTERIOR DESIGN

Susan Fredman & Associates, Ltd.

(left and below) In a room that reverberates with color and youthful energy, an antique sideboard's lean, well-defined look harmonizes with clean-lined contemporary furniture. The sideboard's lack of applied molding is typical of the Federal era.

INTERIOR DESIGN
Marcia Connors and Roxy Gray, Growing Spaces

Photo: Steve Vierra

(above) A glass-top table with
an antique pierced stone sculp-
ture set on a large hammered
copper vase is the focal point of
this breakfast room.

INTERIOR DESIGN
Arlis Ede Interiors, Inc.

(left) An odd shaped room lacking any architectural features was transformed into an eclectic retreat for a world traveler by the design and addition of arches, beams, corbels, and an antique French limestone fireplace. The awkwardly proportional window was enhanced into a focal point by the custom designed Palladian arched shutter treatment.

INTERIOR DESIGN

Barbara Ostrom Associates

(left) For young clients with a collection of very strong twentieth-century paintings, the objective was to achieve clarity of line and simplicity of form by using early nineteenth and twentieth century furniture with simple material.

INTERIOR DESIGN

Brian J. McCarthy, Inc.

(above) INTERIOR DESIGN
Douglas Associates, Inc.

Photo: David Livingston

(right) Wide antique floor boards with distressed charm, handmade Windsor chairs (available through Lynn Robinson Interiors) and an old hutch in a hand-painted soft plaid breakfast room is cozy with a dressed-down sophistication.

INTERIOR DESIGN
Lynn Robinson Interiors

(above) Classic seaside charm in a
breakfast room with blue and white
sunflower fabric-covered walls and
a black Portuguese needlepoint rug
decorated with fruit and flowers.

INTERIOR DESIGN
Diamond Barratta Design, Inc.

(right) INTERIOR DESIGN

Arlene Semel & Associates, Inc.

(right) A custom contemporary limestone fireplace pays homage to traditional details and serves as an anchor for the dramatic Bruce Brainard painting.

INTERIOR DESIGN

Gandy/Peace, Inc.

(above) INTERIOR DESIGN

Noha & Associates

Photo: Jon Miller, Hedrich Blessing

(above) A custom glass, lucite and marble table enhances this elegant dining room.

INTERIOR DESIGN
Fran Murphy & Associates

Photo: Rob Katanis

(right) Old World tile enlivens a small flower sink.

INTERIOR DESIGN
Henry Johnstone & Co.

(above) Ceiling beams from an old barn, darkly stained wood blinds, and antiqued tile floor and blue cabinets recreate the look of a spacious Normandy farmhouse kitchen. In the background is a nineteenth-century French, authentic signed Horloge tall case clock.

INTERIOR DESIGN

Meadowbank Designs Inc.

(left) This fully functional home office is tucked into the corner of a family room. The monitor is recessed into the wall, the printer is closeted underneath, the computer and disks are in the cabinet on the right, and the keyboard and mouse pad fold into the drawer. Everything is instantly accessible—and easily concealed.

(below) Featured on the September '95 cover of *House Beautiful*, this cheerful kitchen and family room are furnished for flexibility. Antique cabinets conceal the refrigerator (left background). *Reprinted by permission from* House Beautiful, *copyright © September 1995. The Heart Corporation. All rights reserved.*

INTERIOR DESIGN

Nancy Mullan, ASID, CKD

Photographer: Richard Felber

(above) Cool, aquatic themes recur throughout this beachside residence, rendering the mood peaceful and the aesthetics powerful.

INTERIOR DESIGN
Eberlein Design Consultants Ltd.

(left) INTERIOR DESIGN

Muriel Hebert, Inc.

Photo: John Vaughan

(below) INTERIOR DESIGN

Muriel Hebert, Inc.

Photo: Jay Graham

(right) Octagonal, turreted ceiling transforms a breakfast room from the practical to the entertaining. A space designed for warm welcomes, with white-washed oak ceiling and cabinetry in play with porcelain and the custom lead glass.

INTERIOR DESIGN

Diane Wendell Interior Design

(left) Generously proportioned
French doors invite the outdoors
to share in the casual comfort of
a cozy sun room.

INTERIOR DESIGN
Carol R. Knott Interior Design

(left) A new kitchen and pantry
was designed with a colonial
revival feeling for a stately
Westchester home.

INTERIOR DESIGN

Diamond Barratta Design, Inc.

(above) In this penthouse dining
room, the screens are adapted
from originals on the Cotê
d'Azur, the sconces are from
Old Palm Beach, the chandelier
is nineteenth-century French, and
the art is by Julian Schnabel.

INTERIOR DESIGN
Barbara Lazarus

(left) A small dining room is visually enlarged with a new bay window and rich blue color on the walls and custom rug. A lovely floral border defines the doorways and walls. The elaborately detailed window treatment adds a formal touch, while echoing the lightness of the chair fabrics. Each piece of china and stemware was painstakingly chosen to repeat the colors.

INTERIOR DESIGN
Susie Leader Interiors, Inc.

(left) Through the use of antique baskets, European wall tiles, and original barn beams, a commodious kitchen with the charm of a European country cottage was created for an active family.

INTERIOR DESIGN
Meadowbank Designs Inc.

(right) INTERIOR DESIGN

Akins and Aylesworth, Ltd.

(below) The design for this New York City dining room addresses the client's love for dramatic and vigorous entertaining. The wall and curtain colors originate in the antique tabriz carpet. The walls are glazed in a navy blue cross-hatched pattern and lacquered to a high gloss finish that reflects a candlelit room.

INTERIOR DESIGN

David Ripp Incorporated

(above) A magnificent dining
room set for dessert invites one
to relax in soft pink tones. A
regal frieze at the ceiling
enhances the room.

INTERIOR DESIGN
James R. Irving, ASID

(below) A painting from realist Mary Sims enhances a John's Island (Florida) residence.

INTERIOR DESIGN

Rodgers Menzies Interior Design

Photo: Rob Katanis

(right) The custom-designed table and chair play off the fabric on the seat pads. A blue arch frames the breakfast area and adds a degree of intensity.

INTERIOR DESIGN

Gail Adams Interiors Ltd.

(left) Timeless elegance marks a dining room that incorporates antique urns on the table to create balance and harmony.

INTERIOR DESIGN

Maha Jano Interiors

(above) Arresting sapphire blue
provides the foundation for a
regal dining room where inlaid
marble harmonizes with silver
leaf and weathered metal.

INTERIOR DESIGN

Eberlein Design Consultants Ltd.

(above) The owner's passion for collecting
all kinds of artwork is reflected in this
colorful conteporary bedroom.

Photo: Bedroom by Dakota Jackson

(above) Good color pairings can often be taken straight from nature. Here, peach and green bring a balance of warm and cool notes to a sunny room.

Bedroom by Cassina

(right) INTERIOR DESIGN

In-Site Design Group Inc.

(above) INTERIOR DESIGN

Bedroom by B & B Italia

(right) A bath in a Victorian house, showing white architectural details against a ground of classic French wallpaper.

INTERIOR DESIGN
Tonin MacCallum ASID, Inc.

(right) The mix of checked, plaid and floral prints in this bedroom work together because they share blue colors of the same value and saturation.

INTERIOR DESIGN
Brunschwig & Fils

(above) With its exuberant fluidity, tropical botanical fabric maintains a crispness that works well with the time-honored styling of the chairs and lamps. The fabric design is by Josef Frank, one of the founders of Swedish Modernism.

Photo courtesy of Brunschwig & Fils

(below) This scheme is essentially monochromatic, but is stimulating to the eye because of the rich combination of dark blue, bright blue, and subtle gray. The solid colors give the sculptural lines of the contemporary furniture crisp definition.

INTERIOR DESIGN

Bedroom by Cassina

(above) Bedrooms have become
daring, with a full spectrum of
color applied in new and exciting
ways.

INTERIOR DESIGN
Bedroom by Cassina

(above) The master bedroom is done
in ocean blues. Unlined silk curtains
catch the summer breeze. An antique
"friendship quilt" covers the foot of the
New England four-poster bed, and a
pair of Gould hummingbird prints
serve as a reminder that the real ones
are just outside.

INTERIOR DESIGN
Jean P. Simmers, Ltd.

(above) INTERIOR DESIGN

Mario Buatta Incorporated

(right) A cobalt blue Santa Fe motif accents the gray stucco walls of a small bath. The bump-out lavatory with recessed base allows for ample storage without taking up half the room. Sophisticated touches to an otherwise whimsical theme are added through the ceramic tile border in the shower and custom chrome hardware.

INTERIOR DESIGN

Jackie Naylor Interiors, Inc.

(right) Blue glazed walls and taffeta lined organdy curtains provide a soothing backdrop to this bedroom where old and new come together.

INTERIOR DESIGN

Barbara Lazarus

(above) INTERIOR DESIGN

Richard Trimble & Associates, Inc.

(below) Elegant silks, brilliant botanical chintz and simple bed linens team up to provide a fascinating combination of fabrics.

INTERIOR DESIGN

Rodgers Menzies Interior Design

(above) A canopy of lace adorns
this four-poster bed in this very
elegantly appointed bedroom.
Archways were created here to
delineate the sitting and dressing
areas from the sleeping area of
the generously sized master
bedroom suite.

INTERIOR DESIGN
Interior Consultants

(above) An elegant and comfortable
master bedroom suite for a home
designed in the eighteenth-century
French style. The room evokes a
Scandinavian influence.

INTERIOR DESIGN
Diamond Barratta Design, Inc.

(above and opposite page)
Grand scale and luxurious
textures combine to create a
spectacular master bath.

INTERIOR DESIGN

Ginny Stine Interiors, Inc.

(above) A hideaway for young boys or a future astronomer comprises stars, suns, and moons on the walls and windows. The sturdy bunk beds and desk are both fun and functional and add to the element of nature.

INTERIOR DESIGN
Sue Wenk Interior Design Inc.

(above) Warmth, charm, and
subtle elegance are the hallmarks
of this inviting master bedroom.
Magnificent fabrics and outstand-
ing architectural details complete
the picture.

INTERIOR DESIGN
Joan Polk Interiors

(above) The mingling of period
pieces, warmth and charm, and
the use of exciting fabrics and
colors are reminiscent of a time
gone by.

INTERIOR DESIGN
Joan Polk Interiors

(right) INTERIOR DESIGN

Barbara Jacobs Interior Design

Photo: Russell Abraham

(above) This triad scheme using tints of primary colors is a case study in color harmony. The values are relatively equal; no single color is more dominant than another. Because blue, yellow, and red are equidistant on the color wheel, this combination of tints is soothing but quietly enlivening as well.

Photo: Steve Vierra

(above) All references to the usual tile
look have been removed in this bath
by adopting a deeper version of the
colors in the adjacent study/bedroom.
A paneled screen hinged like a door
has been utilized to shield the toilet
area from view.

INTERIOR DESIGN
Interior Options

(below) Vibrant cool blue walls pronounce the red antique painted furniture and add depth to the room. Crisp blue and white fabrics from Cowtan & Tout and accents of red maintain the integrity of the atmosphere.

INTERIOR DESIGN

Elizabeth Read Weber, ASID, LLC

(above) Sunlight from the east
floods an exquisite master bath
that's perhaps better described
as a "private morning room."

INTERIOR DESIGN
Gus Duffy A.I.A. Architect

(below) INTERIOR DESIGN

Riemenschneider Design Associates, Inc.

(above) The use of saturated color
and zebra upholstery create a
sense of mystery in this historic
bedroom.

INTERIOR DESIGN

Wagner Van Dam Design & Decoration

~ Directory ~

Akins & Aylesworth, Ltd.
26 East First Street
Hinsdale, IL 60521
630/325.3355
Fax: 630/325.3315

Al Evans Interiors
1001 South Bayshore Drive # 2902
Miami, FL 33131

Alexis E. Benné Interiors
100 Riverside Drive
New York, NY 10024
212/580.8118
Fax: 212/769.0809

Arlene Semel & Associates, Inc.
445 N. Franklin
Chicago, IL 60610
312/644.1480
Fax: 312/644.8157

Arlis Ede Interiors, Inc.
3520 Fairmount
Dallas, TX 75219
214/521.1302
Fax: 214/559.4729

B & B Italia, USA, Inc.
150 East 58th Street
Architects and Designers Building
New York, NY 10155

Barbara Jacobs Interior Design
12340 Saratoga-Sunnyvale Road
Saratoga, CA 95070
408/446.2225
Fax: 408/446.2607

Barbara Lazarus
10 Fones Alley
Providence, RI 02906
401/521.8910
Fax: 401/438.8809

Barbara Ostrom Associates
One International Plaza
Mahwah, NJ 07495
201/529.0444
Fax: 201/529.0449
and
55 East 87 Street
New York, NY 10128
212/465.1808

Blair Design Associates
315 West 78th Street
New York, NY 10024
212/595.0203
Fax: 212/595.0245
e-mail: blairdesign@msn.com

Brian J. McCarthy, Inc.
1414 Avenue of the Americas
Suite 404
New York, NY 10019
212/308.7600
Fax: 212/308.4242

Brunschwig & Fils
979 Third Avenue
New York, NY 10022

C.M. Wright, Inc.
700 N. La Cienega Boulevard
Los Angeles, CA 90069
310/657.7655
Fax: 310/657.4440

Carl Steele Associates
1606 Pine Street
Philadelphia, PA 19103
215/546.5530
Fax: 215/546.1571

Carol R. Knott Interior Design
430 Green Bay Road
Kenilworth, IL 60043
847/256.6676
Fax: 847/256.6689

Cassina USA
200 McKay Road
Huntington Station, NY 11746

Dakota Jackson
979 Third Avenue, Suite 503
New York, NY 10022

David Ripp Incorporated
215 West 84th Street
New York, NY 10024
212/362.7706
Fax: 212/362.4486
e-mail: dugancastle@worldnet.att.net

Dennis Rolland Inc.
405 East 54th Street
New York, NY 10022
212/644.0537
Fax: 212/486.9189

Diamond Baratta Design Inc.
270 Lafayette Street
New York, NY 10012
212/966.8892
Fax: 212/966.4261

Diane Wendell Interior Design
1121 Warren Avenue
Downers Grove, IL 60515
630/852.0235
Fax: 630/968.8341

Douglas Associates, Inc.
2525 E. Exposition Avenue
Denver, CO 80209
303/722.6979
Fax: 303/722.9663

Eberlein Design Consultants, Ltd.
1809 Walnut Street, Suite 410
Philadelphia, PA 19103
215/405.0400
Fax: 215/405.0588

Elizabeth Read Weber, LLC
79 East Putnam Avenue
Greenwich, CT 06830
203/869.5659
Fax: 203/869.3778
e-mail: erwllc@aol.com

Fetzer's Interiors
711 Jefferson Highway
Baton Rouge, LA 70806
504/927.7420
Fax: 504/927.8280

Fran Murphy & Associates
71 E. Allendale Road
Saddle River, NJ 07458
201/934.6029
Fax: 201/934.5597
e-mail: enm2@worldnet.att.net

Gail Adams Interiors, Ltd.
110 East San Miguel
Phoenix, AZ 85012
602/274.0074
Fax: 602/274.8897

Gandy/Peace, Inc.
349 Peachtree Hills Avenue NE
Suite C-2
Atlanta, GA 30350
404/237.8681
Fax: 404/237.6150
charlesgandy@mindspring.com

Ginny Stine Interiors
1936 Marco Boulevard
Jacksonville, FL 32207
904/396.9814
Fax: 904/398.3175

G. M. Doveikis & Associates, Inc.
2058 Concourse Drive
St. Louis, MO 63146
314/567.4944
Fax: 314/537.9629
e-mail: gmdanda@aol.com

Growing Spaces
Marcia Connors & Roxy Gray
4 Fall Lane
Canton, MA 02021

Gus Duffy Architect
11333 Moorpark Street, Box 455
Toluca Lake, CA 91602
818/509.0505
Fax: 818/509.7847
e-mail: gduffy@pacbell.net

Henry Johnstone & Co.
95 San Miguel Road
Pasadena, CA 91105
818/716.7624
Fax: 818/716.0017

Horne International Designs, Inc.
5272 River Road, Suite 450
Bethesda, MD 20816
301/656.4304
Fax: 301/907.0258

In-Site Design Group
3551 S. Monaco Parkway
Denver, CO 80237
303/691.9000
Fax: 303/757.6475

Interior Consultants
21 Fox Run
South Salem, NY 10590
914/533.2275
Fax: 914/533.2276
e-mail: dbala@ix.netcom.com

Interior Options
200 Lexington Avenue, Suite 420
New York, NY 10016
212/726.9708
Fax: 212/689.4064

Jackie Naylor Interiors, Inc.
4287 Glengary Drive
Atlanta, GA 30342
404/814.1973
Fax: 404/814.1973

James R. Irving ASID
13901 Shaker Boulevard
Cleveland, OH 44120
216/283.1991

Jane J. Marsden Antiques & Interiors, Inc.
2300 Peachtree Road, 102A
Atlanta, GA 30309
404/355.1288
Fax: 404/355.4552

Jean P. Simmers, Ltd.
24 Smith Street
Rye, NY 10580
914/967.8533
Fax: 914/967.6085

J. Westerfield Antiques & Interiors, Inc.
4429 Old Canton Road
Jackson, MS 39211
601/362.7508
Fax: 601/366.4718

Judith Lynne Interior Design
PO Box 4998
Palm Springs, CA 92263
760/324.7606
Fax: 760/328.8190

Julie Lanterman Interior Designs
5 St. Francis Road
Hillsborough, CA 94010
650/348.3823
Fax: 650/348.3823

Lynn Robinson Interiors
Powers Building, 34 Audrey Avenue
Oyster Bay, NY 11771
516/921.4455
Fax: 516/921.8163

Maha Jano Interiors
1700 Stutz, Suite 102B
Troy, MI 48084
248/816.8044
Fax: 248/647.5618

Mario Buatta Inc.
120 East 80th Street
New York, NY 10021
212/988.6811
Fax: 212/861.9321

Mary W. Delaney Interior Design
1 Strawberry Hill Court
Stamford, CT 06902
203/348.6839
Fax: 203/324.7229

Meadowbank Designs Inc.
Box 168
Bryn Mawr, PA 19010
610/525.4909
Fax: 610/525.3909

Muriel Hebert Interiors
117 Sheridan Avenue
Piedmont, CA 94611
510/547.1294
Fax: 510/655.1509

Nancy Mullen
NDM Kitchens Inc.
204 E. 77 Street
New York, NY 10021
212/628.4629
Fax: 212/628.6738

Noha & Associates, Inc.
1735 W. Fletcher
Chicago, IL 60657
773/549.1414
Fax: 773/549.1479

Peter Charles Associates, Ltd.
17 East Main Street
Oyster Bay, NY 11771
516/624.9276
Fax: 516/625.9367

Rhonda A. Roman Interiors
2148 Seminole
Detroit, MI 48214
313/924.6877
Fax: 313/921.9378

Trimble & Assoc. Inc.
6517 Hillcrest, Suite 310
Dallas, TX 75205
214/363.2283
Fax: 214/363.6364

Riemenschneider Design Associates, Inc.
122 S. Main Street, Suite 355
Ann Arbor, MI 48106
313/930.0882
Fax: 313/930.0974
e-mail: alyce@riedesign.com

Rita St. Clair Associates
1009 N. Charles Street
Baltimore, MD 21201
410/752.1313
Fax: 410/752.1335

Robert E. Tartarini Interiors
P.O. Box 293
Old Westbury, NY 11568

Robert Pope Associates, Inc.
400 N. Wells Street, #400
Chicago, IL 60610
312/527.2077
Fax: 312/527.2079
e-mail: rpopeassoc@aol.com

Rodgers Menzies Interior Design
766 South White Station Road
Memphis, TN 38117
901/761.3161
Fax: 901/763.3993

Ronald Bricke & Associates, Inc.
333 East 69th Street, #7B
New York, NY 10021
212/472.9006
Fax: 212/472.9008
e-mail: rbricke@aol.com

Sara Zook Designs
2001A Youngfield
Golden, CO 80401
303/237.4544
Fax: 303/237.1647

Solis Betancourt
1054 Potomac Street, NW
Washington, DC 20007
202/659.8734
Fax: 202/659.0035

Stedila Design
135 East 55th Street
New York, NY 10022
212/751.4281
Fax: 212/751.6698

Sue Wenk
300 East 71st Street
Newy York, NY 10021
212/879.5149

Susan Fredman & Associates, Ltd.
1510 Old Deerfield Road
Highland Park, IL 60035
847/831.1419
Fax: 847/831.0719

Susie Leader Interiors
1280 Latham
Birmingham, MI 48009
248/642.2571
Fax: 248/642.9897
e-mail: suleaderi@aol.com

Tomar Lampert Associates
8900 Melrose Avenue, Suite 202
Los Angeles, CA 90069
310/271.4299
Fax: 310/271.1569

Tonin MacCallum ASID, Inc.
21 E. 90
New York City, NY 10128
212/831.8909
Fax: 212/427.2069

Wagner Van Dam Design
853 Broadway
New York, NY 10005
212/674.3070
Fax: 212/995.9861

William R. Eubanks Interior Design
1516 Union Avenue
Memphis, TN 38104
901/272.1825
Fax: 901/272.1845

~ Index ~